RECYCLING

Think about a world with no rubbish. Food goes back onto the land and helps to grow more food. Old vegetable oil makes the buses run, and two old bicycles make one new bicycle. When you don't want something, you give it to somebody else.

Now think about a world full of rubbish. Animals and fish eat our plastic bags and die. Ships full of toxic waste go from country to country, but nobody wants them. We think that we throw things away – but there are fewer and fewer places to put the rubbish.

Decide to recycle, and you can help to make a cleaner, more pleasant world. Just turn the page, and you can learn how to start saving electricity, trees, the environment – and money!

OXFORD BOOKWORMS LIBRARY

Factfiles

Recycling

Stage 3 (1000 headwords)

Factfiles Series Editor: Christine Lindop

SUE STEWART

Recycling

OXFORD UNIVERSITY PRESS

OXFORD
UNIVERSITY PRESS

Great Clarendon Street, Oxford OX2 6DP

Oxford University Press is a department of the University of Oxford.
It furthers the University's objective of excellence in research, scholarship,
and education by publishing worldwide in

Oxford New York

Auckland Cape Town Dar es Salaam Hong Kong Karachi
Kuala Lumpur Madrid Melbourne Mexico City Nairobi
New Delhi Shanghai Taipei Toronto

With offices in

Argentina Austria Brazil Chile Czech Republic France Greece
Guatemala Hungary Italy Japan Poland Portugal Singapore
South Korea Switzerland Thailand Turkey Ukraine Vietnam

OXFORD and OXFORD ENGLISH are registered trade marks of
Oxford University Press in the UK and in certain other countries

ISBN: 978 0 19 423389 7

A complete recording of this Bookworms edition of *Recycling*
is available on audio CD ISBN 978 0 19 423598 3

Printed in China

This book is printed on paper from certified and well-managed sources.

Word count (main text): 10098

For more information on the Oxford Bookworms
Library, visit www.oup.com/bookworms

The publishers would like to thank the following for permission to reproduce images:
africanpictures.net p 23 (children with cars/Guy Stubbs); Alamy Images pp 1 (Si Barber), 11 (Gari
Wyn Williams), 12 (Jeff Greenberg), 14 (Jim West), 18 (Paul Ridsdale), 23 (tin can toy aeroplane/
EggImages), 23 (tin can toy car/EggImages), 40 (Julio Etchart), 42 (Sue Heaton), 47 (Ashley Cooper),
48 (Ashley Cooper), 50 (TRG); Corbis pp 4 (Gianni Dagli Orti), 6 (Joseph Sohm/Visions of America),
8 (Swansea, 1944/Hulton-Deutsch Collection), 9 (Peter Turnley), 10 (Brad Simmons/Beateworks), 17
(Bettmann), 26 (Gabe Palmer), 36 (Art on File), 41 (Owen Franken), 46 (Peter Johnson), 54 (Herve
Collart/Sygma); Ecoscene p 21 (Robert Nichol); EcoCentric p 34; Copyright Freecycle p 55; Getty
Images pp viii (Robb Kendrick/Aurora), 19 (Bavaria/Taxi), 44 (ChinaFotoPress); Copyright Jeff Clapp
38; Copyright Martin Hill p 56; PA Photos p 3 (Christian Aslund/Greenpeace/AP); Panos Pictures p 30
(Azerbaijan/Gerd Ludwig, Visum); Photolibrary p 51 (Mel Watson); PunchStock p 52 (BananaStock);
Rex Features p 33 (EcoCentric room/Nils Jorgensen); Still Pictures p 28 (Pakistan/Mark Edwards);
Thames21 p 24; View p 29 (Duracell/Jeff Goldberg)

CONTENTS

1 The rubbish problem

What is rubbish and what happens to it? It is not something that people like to think about too often. When we throw away our rubbish, we usually forget about it. Somebody takes it away and it is not our problem any more. Or is it?

What happens to the rubbish that everyone throws away every week? Where does it go? Why should people recycle rubbish? Why not just put it into the bin?

The fact is that there is not enough room for everybody's rubbish any more. A lot of rubbish goes into big holes in the ground called landfill sites, but after a time these fill up. Finding new landfill sites is a problem nearly everywhere in the world.

So why is this happening? How much rubbish do we throw away? Here are some facts about rubbish.

- 8 billion plastic bags are used in the UK each year, and most of them are only used once and then thrown away. That is 135 bags for each person in a year.
- In Hong Kong customers use 6.7 million bags a year – 1,294 plastic bags for each person.
- In Greece plastic from landfill sites gets into the sea and kills 10,000 fish each day.
- In South Africa the wind has blown thousands of plastic bags into the trees, and people now call plastic bags 'the new South African flower'.
- In the UK 1.5 million computers are put into landfill sites each year.
- Japan has over 600 landfill sites but many of them are nearly full.
- During the Christmas holidays of 2005, people in UK homes put 550 million glass bottles into their rubbish bins.
- In the USA each person throws away about 2 kilos of rubbish a day.

So why don't we just burn our rubbish? Burning rubbish sounds like a good idea but there are problems. If you burn rubbish, it can make unpleasant smoke which is bad for people's health. People who live near the fires can become very ill, so burning rubbish is not the best answer.

How do you throw away a television or a battery or an old car? This kind of rubbish is called toxic waste. It contains things – perhaps metals or chemicals – that can be dangerous for people and animals. They can also be very bad for the land, the rivers, and the sea. Most countries in the world have laws about toxic waste. Usually these laws say that

A toxic ship

you have to take toxic waste to a special place where the dangerous things can be removed safely. The problem is that this process is very expensive and difficult.

In the past, some countries decided to give the problem to someone else. Rich countries put their toxic waste into old ships and paid poorer countries to take it. But after a time the poorer countries began to say no to this dangerous rubbish. Toxic ships began to sail around the world. They tried to stop at one country after another but nobody wanted them.

So every day all over the world the problem of rubbish gets bigger. For rich countries and for poor countries it is a terrible problem.

Has anybody got an answer? There are some countries in the world that do not make very much rubbish. There are people in some parts of Mexico who do not have a word for 'rubbish' in their language. Why not? The reason is that they do not have any rubbish. They do not know what rubbish is. For them, everything is useful, and everything can be used more than once. They recycle everything. And this is not a new idea. The story of recycling began a long time ago.

2   5,000 years of rubbish and recycling

In the earliest times there were no towns. People lived in small groups and often moved from place to place while they looked for wild animals that they could kill and eat. They did not have much rubbish, only ash from their fires and bits of old food. All of this was put into the ground and it probably helped their vegetables to grow better.

The problem of waste began when people started to live in towns. The earliest landfill sites were found in Knossos,

An early landfill site

the capital of Crete, and these were probably made in about 3000 BC. These very old sites in Crete are different from the landfill sites of today and contain mostly ash, wood, and pieces of plates and bowls.

Over 2,500 years ago the government of Athens said they did not want a landfill site in the city. They told the people of Athens that they had to take all their rubbish outside the city walls, about two kilometres outside Athens. This is the first story about the problem of waste that we know of.

It is a problem that began a very long time ago, but even then people were finding answers. In China in 2000 BC, for example, people composted their rubbish. This means that they put all their bits of old vegetables and fruit in one place outside and left it there. After a few months it changed into a rich brown material called compost, which is very good for plants. They used this compost to grow young plants in the garden. Many gardeners today still like to make compost and use it in their gardens. It is an old idea but a good one! Maybe composting is the first example of recycling.

But it is not worth making compost if you do not have a garden. In England people who lived in towns just used to throw their rubbish outside the door. Sometimes there was a lot of rubbish outside the houses and it became difficult to walk along the streets. The streets also smelt very bad. In 1297 the government said they would punish people who left rubbish in front of their houses, but nobody cared about this. They burnt some of their rubbish on the fires inside their houses, but they continued to throw the rest outside onto the streets.

In London the streets became very dirty and sometimes it was impossible to walk in them. When people went outside they wore high shoes made of wood to try to keep their feet clean. Sometimes the rubbish was taken out of London and thrown away in the country. At last in 1354 the government began to employ special workers to take the rubbish away.

In Germany at the same time a clever idea helped to get rubbish out of the cities. People came to the towns with carts full of fruit and vegetables. They sold the food in the markets and went home in the evening with empty carts. A new law said that people must leave at the end of the day with their carts full of rubbish to carry away to the country. Nobody could leave with an empty cart.

Making compost

Shoes for walking in dirty streets

In England the government now began to punish people who threw their rubbish onto the streets. People everywhere know about William Shakespeare, England's most famous writer. But not many people know that his father broke the law. In 1515 he threw rubbish into the street and was punished for it. He had to pay some money to the government. Shakespeare, of course, did not write about this!

But the world's biggest problems with rubbish began when machines and factories were built. Now rubbish came from factories as well as from people's houses. At the same time many people left their villages and came to live and work in the towns, so the towns got bigger and dirtier. There were many diseases in towns and often people died when they were very young. Doctors said that many diseases came from dirty houses and rubbish.

In the UK in 1848 the government made a new law called the Public Health Act. Now people were employed to take away the rubbish from every town. By the end of the nineteenth century it was taken away every day. Some of it was then recycled and used to make new things such as soap or paper. Other rubbish was just left in big dirty hills outside the towns.

Some recycling jobs were not very pleasant. For example there were people who lived and worked beside rivers. They looked in or near the water for rubbish which they could sell. But the work was cold and difficult and they did not get

Factories brought more problems

much money for the things that they found. Others had an even worse job. In the nineteenth century there were people who lived and worked in the underground pipes that take away the dirty water from big cities. Their work was dangerous and very smelly, but sometimes they were lucky and found bits of metal or even coins and gold. Other very poor people lived near the big landfill sites where rubbish was taken from the towns. They tried to find things like old clothes or bits of metal to sell.

Even today there are people who make their money from rubbish. In a poor part of Cairo a group of people called the Zabbaleen live with their pigs and goats. They go out to people's houses with small carts and take away their rubbish, which they bring back to their villages.

What do they do with all this rubbish? They sort it and take out everything that is useful. They sell plastic, paper, wood, and metal, which can be reused or recycled. When they find bits of old food, they give it to their pigs and goats. Later they can eat or sell these animals. The Zabbaleen collect about 35 per cent of Cairo's rubbish, and they recycle as much as 80 per cent of it.

Life near a landfill site is dirty and difficult, but for thousands of people near some of the world's biggest cities it is the only way of life that they know. It is also dangerous and unhealthy. People can get diseases from the rubbish, and babies born near the sites often have health problems. Sometimes there are terrible accidents too.

In the Philippines people have built small houses out of bits of wood and metal next to the landfill sites near Manila. Every day families climb up the hills of 'new' rubbish when it arrives from Manila. They look for plastic, paper, wood, glass, metal, anything that they can sell. Everybody in the family has to work, and children as young as four years old climb the rubbish hills with their parents. In July 2000, at a site called Payatas near Manila, one of the hills got too big. People were climbing on it when it fell onto the village and started a fire, which destroyed many houses. Hundreds of people died under the burning rubbish. Yet, even after that terrible accident, people still live at Payatas and continue to search through the rubbish. Without it, they have no job and no money.

The Zabbaleen at work

3 Our throwaway world

Recycling is a modern word, but it is not a modern idea. In the past people sometimes recycled rubbish to make money. Very poor people collected things that other people threw away and then sold them, and this still happens in some places.

But in the past there was not as much rubbish as there is today. When people bought or made things, they tried to

Made to last

keep them for a very long time and then they gave them to their children. The same plates, chairs, and farm carts were used by families for many, many years.

Today it is very different. Something which is new one year becomes old the next year. Examples of this are cars, phones, and computers, which change very quickly. Many things that people use every day are made of cheap metal or plastic. They get broken very quickly and it is easy to buy new ones. In fact it is much easier to buy new ones than to find someone who can repair things for you.

And then there is the question of money. Businesses make more money from things that people use once or just for a short time, because they can sell more of them. They can also sell more if they change the shape and colour of the things that they make. If last year's phone or TV looks old and out of date, people will throw it away and buy a new one, because they want to be fashionable.

Made to throw away

Packaging

So people go shopping a lot. They like to have new things, and they also like their new things to look beautiful. Sometimes they decide to buy something because it comes in a very big, brightly coloured box with lots of plastic inside. Packaging like this makes ordinary things look better. Businesses like packaging because it makes things look more expensive, and that means a higher price.

One example of expensive packaging is children's toys. Sometimes the packaging is more interesting than the toy inside it. Small children often play with the box and leave the toy on the floor!

In Japan many shops like to sell things with plenty of paper and plastic and pretty boxes. When customers buy apples, each apple has its own plastic cover on it. If you buy carrots in the supermarket, sometimes there is special packaging for each carrot!

People today often say that we live in a 'throwaway world'. Customers buy things and throw away the packaging. Or they quickly get bored with the thing that they have bought and they look for something different. But what happens to the things that they throw away? In the United States each person throws away 2 kilos of rubbish a day, but in 1960 it was only 1 kilo. (The United States throws away more rubbish than any other country in the world, but 80 per cent of this rubbish can be reused or recycled.) So people throw away more and more things, and the mountains of rubbish get bigger and bigger.

This used to be a problem in only a few countries but now it happens nearly everywhere. All over the world people's ideas are changing. In China twenty years ago most people went to work by bicycle, but now they want cars. They also want new phones, televisions, and the most fashionable clothes and sports shoes. Like everybody else they buy new things and throw away the old things.

The problem of rubbish is getting worse every year as more and more countries join the throwaway world. What is the answer?

The UK is a small country, but it puts 80 per cent of its rubbish into landfill sites. Greece is even worse – more than 90 per cent of its rubbish goes into landfill sites. But we know that landfill sites are getting full. Smaller countries like the UK cannot make any more landfill sites because there is nowhere to put them. They are dangerous, unhealthy places too.

Burning rubbish

People used to think that burning rubbish was a good idea. It was fast and easy and it made the rubbish much smaller. But burning rubbish is expensive, and the ash from the fires is dangerous as well as the smoke. In the past people used the ash to make roads and parks, but then they discovered that it made people ill. They stopped using it to make roads and just put it into landfill sites instead. Of course this made the landfill sites even more dangerous than before.

So what can we do to change our throwaway world? Perhaps the answer is recycling. People have always used rubbish to make money, but the difference is that now people are recycling rubbish to save the Earth. Recycling is cleaner and better for the environment than landfill sites or burning.

In many countries governments are beginning to make laws about recycling rubbish. But some countries are better at it than others. In the UK the landfill sites have grown bigger by 3 per cent a year since 1999, but recycling has only grown by 1 per cent. The UK only recycles 12.4 per cent of its rubbish, but Austria recycles 64 per cent, Belgium 52 per cent, and the Netherlands 47 per cent. And Switzerland only puts 7 per cent of its rubbish into landfill sites.

How do you change a throwaway world into a recycling world? You begin at the beginning – with the things that are easy to recycle.

4   Glass and paper

In richer countries people throw away more and more rubbish every year. In poorer countries there is less rubbish, but in some places there is nobody to take it away, so it just lies in the streets.

But a lot of things that we throw away can be used again or recycled. In fact many governments are now asking people to do this.

What kinds of things can be recycled? The answer is, nearly everything. Let us look at some of the things that people are recycling. We can start with the easiest, which is glass.

Glass was first used in about 4000 BC in the Middle East. People made jewellery from very small coloured glass balls and wore it around their necks. Clear glass – glass with no colour, like the glass used in windows – was first made in about 800 BC in Nineveh (now the city of Mosul in Iraq). Glass was expensive until the eighteenth and nineteenth centuries so nobody threw it away. Even in the twentieth century people used glass bottles again and again. In the UK until recently most people bought their milk from the milkman. He left full bottles of milk outside people's houses and took away the empty ones. These were then washed at the factory and then they were used again. Children also used to take empty drinks bottles back to shops and get a little money for each bottle.

In the UK today every family uses around 330 glass bottles each year, but they do not usually take them back to the

Milk in bottles from the milkman

shop. Although some families still leave glass milk bottles outside their front doors for the milkman, most people just buy milk in plastic bottles from the supermarket.

New Zealand is another country where people have mostly stopped buying from the milkman and get their milk from the supermarket instead. But in New Zealand today the Green Party want to save the glass milk bottle. A milk bottle, they say, is much better than a plastic bottle or a box. A milk bottle can be washed and used as many as twenty times, but plastic bottles usually go straight to landfill sites.

Glass is easy to recycle. There are three kinds of glass: clear glass, green glass, and brown glass. They cannot be recycled together so there are often three different bins for glass, one for each colour. The glass is broken into very small pieces which are heated until they become liquid. Then they are made into new bottles which can be used again in the shops.

Why is it good to recycle glass? Recycling one glass bottle saves enough electricity to make your TV work for one and a half hours!

Recycling glass

Recycling paper

Some countries recycle more glass than others. Switzerland and Finland each recycle more than 90 per cent of their glass bottles but the UK only recycles 34 per cent.

If you look inside a landfill site you will find that nearly 40 per cent of the rubbish is paper. But paper, like glass, is easy to recycle. Recycling paper is good for the Earth, because you need 64 per cent less electricity and 58 per cent less water than you need to make new paper. It helps to keep forests of older trees alive too. It is easy to grow trees for paper, but they are special kinds of trees that grow quickly. This is not always a good thing. Older trees that grow slowly are often cut down to make room for these new fast-growing trees. The birds and animals that live in the older kinds of trees lose their homes and die, because they cannot live in the new trees.

Many shops sell things made of recycled paper; look for the 'recycled' sign on paper, cards, and other things when you go shopping. But there are also problems when you recycle paper. You cannot do it again and again; after a while you need to add some new paper to the recycled paper to make it strong enough to use. Although recycling paper is good, it is even better to try to use less paper. You can find out how to do this in Chapter 9.

Which country uses the most paper? The answer is the USA. Every day American businesses use enough paper to go round the Earth twenty times! But the USA is trying to recycle more paper too. In 2005 they recycled 45 per cent of their paper, and now they are trying to recycle more than 50 per cent. But they are also using more paper every year so they still have the same problem.

Other countries also use more and more paper each year, especially South East Asia and Japan. But they are also trying to recycle more.

Which countries are good at recycling paper? Switzerland again. Most people in Switzerland recycle everything made of paper, not only newspapers. Another country that recycles its paper is Senegal.

Recycling is part of ordinary life for people in Senegal and many other African countries. Old newspapers and business letters are often used to wrap the bread, fruit, and other food that people buy in the street. Many families have goats. Goats often eat people's rubbish and they do not mind a bit of paper. Maybe goats are the world's best recyclers!

5   Metal and plastic

Metal is another easy thing to recycle. Different kinds of metal are recycled in different ways and in many different countries. It saves money because metal is expensive. Americans use 300 million cans for food and drink *every day*. Luckily they also recycle a lot, so their country does not fill up with old metal.

There are two kinds of metal that can be recycled: aluminium and steel. Cans for beer and other drinks are

Recycling aluminium cans

usually made from aluminium. Steel is used in cans which contain food, such as cans of fish or fruit.

Aluminium is a valuable metal which is found under the ground and then taken to factories. It is quite difficult and expensive to get aluminium out of the ground and make things from it, and it also uses a lot of electricity. It is much cheaper to use recycled aluminium and it saves electricity. The Americans are now very good at recycling aluminium and steel; doing this means that they can save enough electricity to light a big city like Los Angeles for nearly ten years. Aluminium companies in America want people to recycle; they pay a cent for every aluminium container that is recycled.

Aluminium and steel are both very easy to recycle. Old cans are taken to a recycling factory, where machines cut them into very small pieces. The pieces are then heated until they become liquid. The liquid is put into special containers and left there to become cool and hard. It is then made into flat sheets of metal. Aluminium is usually made into drinks containers again. Steel can be made into many different things like cans, bridges, and cars.

Steel and aluminium can both be recycled many times, and unlike paper, they always stay strong.

What do other countries do? Most countries recycle metal. But in some countries like Senegal people are good at re-using metal. In small villages old cans are washed and used as drinks containers. Some people know how to use empty cans to make bowls for the kitchen or children's toys. In Afghanistan the Taliban government did not allow people to buy satellite dishes for their TVs, so people made their own out of old oil containers.

Perhaps the biggest problem in recycling is plastic. Plastic

Toys made from recycled metal

bottles are things we usually use once and then throw away. But plastic bottles can last for 450 years. And people have found very small pieces of plastic on beaches and islands that are a very long way from modern cities.

Plastic is cheap and light and easy to use, so it is very popular. Plastic is used much more today than it was in the past. In the 1950s the whole world used about 5 million tonnes of plastic a year. Today the world uses around 100 million tonnes.

Plastic bags are a real problem. The first plastic bags for shopping were used only about 35 years ago but now the world uses over 500 billion plastic bags a year. The world is full of plastic bags. You can see them everywhere – in the sea, on beaches, beside roads. There are even plastic bags in the trees. In Japan people throw away 30 billion plastic bags each year.

Plastic bags are not very beautiful, and they can make

serious problems for people and animals too. Bangladesh is a very wet country, and in some months of the year sudden heavy rain is not unusual. But the pipes under the streets are often full of plastic bags, so they cannot take the water away. The heavy rain quickly makes deep rivers in the streets. The rainwater fills people's houses and sometimes people die in the deep water.

Plastic bags are very bad for animals too. 100,000 turtles are killed every year by plastic bags. They eat the bags because they think the bags are fish. In fact, plastic is dangerous for fish too, and in the Mediterranean plastic bags kill thousands of fish each day. Other animals eat plastic as well. In India people think that cows are special animals, and you can see cows on the streets of towns as well as in the country. But their life is not as happy today as it was in the past. Now 95 per cent of the cows in India's towns have stomach problems because they have eaten plastic bags. The government in India is now trying to change this, and in some big Indian towns plastic bags cannot be used. Perhaps the cows will be happy and healthy again.

Can plastic be recycled? Yes it can, but it is not easy to do. There are six different kinds of plastic, and they must be sorted into their different groups before the work begins. When plastic is recycled it can be made into many different things. Some examples of these things are winter jackets, parts of cars and garden furniture. In fact it is surprising to discover all the different things that you can do with recycled plastic. But the process is expensive, and most people agree that using less plastic is better than recycling it.

6 Other problems

In the twentieth century many new things like computers and mobile phones changed people's lives and made them easier. But some of these things can damage the Earth if they go into landfill sites. The problem is that people like to change their phones very often. In the UK most people get a new phone every 18 months. That means about 15 million mobile phones are bought every year.

What happens to the old ones? If you put 15 million phones together one on top of the other, you will make a tall, very thin building. This 'building' will be much higher than Mount Everest.

Twentieth-century rubbish

Perhaps this building is not a very good idea, but there are other things you can do with old mobile phones. The best thing to do is to recycle them. In the UK people collect old phones and send them to poorer countries, where other people can use them. Mobile phones are very important in countries where there are not many telephone lines.

Old computers can also be useful. Some groups of people take away old computers and give them to poorer countries. Sometimes they have to mend them first, but afterwards they have a machine that they can use. It is better to mend a computer than to throw it away.

A lot of people are now beginning to realize that the things they throw away are possibly useful for someone else. In the UK there are places where people sell or just give their unwanted things to other people. They leave messages on special websites and tell people that they have things to sell or give away.

Sometimes they just put things outside their houses at night – furniture or books for example. They know that when they get up in the morning their old chair or box of books will not be there any more. Their rubbish will be an exciting surprise for somebody else.

In New Zealand the government asked people to put their rubbish out in the street on a special date. People began to put out their old furniture, boxes, bicycles, and pieces of wood and metal a few days before. When the workers arrived to collect the rubbish, half of it had gone. People had seen things that they wanted and taken them. So there was less rubbish to take away, and a lot of people had found useful things. Reusing things is another kind of recycling.

But what can you do with an old fridge or a broken washing machine? The answer is that governments in Europe

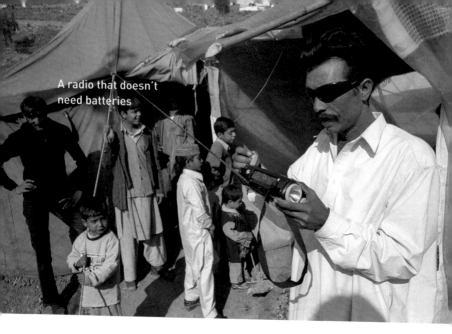
A radio that doesn't need batteries

have now made new laws about this. If a business sells new electrical machines, it must also take away and recycle the old ones. But some people already do this. In many countries of the world people mend all their broken machines. In poorer countries people cannot buy a new fridge or washing machine when an old one is broken, so they have to mend it. In richer countries too some people are starting to think about recycling machines. Renew North East is a place in the north-east of England where washing machines, fridges, and cookers are all recycled and then sold again. They are as good as new machines but they are cheaper.

Many small electrical things work with batteries. But people should not throw batteries away with other rubbish, because they contain toxic waste, and they can also explode in fires. In many countries there are special places where people can take batteries for recycling. But perhaps there are other answers too. Some special kinds of batteries can be used again and again. There are also radios and small lights which do not need batteries. You turn a little wheel on the back of them and they work for about twenty minutes. You do not have to worry about batteries and recycling, because you make the electricity for them yourself! They are also very useful in countries where it is too difficult or too expensive to buy batteries. You can also get lights, radios and other things which use the light from the sun to make electricity.

But now the people who make batteries are beginning to think about recycling too. One of the biggest battery businesses in the world, Duracell, has recently built a new office building. Half of the building is made from recycled rubbish from their own factories. The floor is made of pieces of glass from broken lights. The ceiling is made of squares of painted, recycled newspaper. The roof is made of recycled aluminium.

Oil is another difficult thing to recycle. If you change the oil in your own car engine you have to be careful where you put the old oil. It can damage the Earth, and it is bad for rivers and the sea. So it has to go to special places where people can clean it and recycle it.

Another kind of oil which we throw away is vegetable oil,

The Duracell office building

but perhaps in the future people will recycle this in a different way. In 2003 a group of American students drove their school bus on a long trip across America. What was so special about this journey? The answer is that they used vegetable oil in the engine. They never visited a garage. Instead, every time they got to a town they visited fast-food restaurants and asked for used oil. The restaurant owners were happy to get rid of their old oil. The only problem was the smell.

Oil is bad for rivers and the sea

'Sometimes the bus's engine smelt of chips,' one of the students said. 'And sometimes it smelt of onions or chicken. We always knew what kind of food was cooked in each restaurant. We knew this from the smell of the bus.'

Was the 'vegetable oil bus' a clever idea? Perhaps it was. More and more people are now searching for a way to make cars travel using vegetable oil. It is cheap and good for the Earth too. But perhaps the smell will be a problem!

7   Paper houses and Everest bells

Most people know that it is possible to recycle many things. If you recycle your old glass bottles, people can use them to make new glass bottles. If you recycle plastic bottles, factories can make new bottles from the old plastic. The newspapers you read are probably made from recycled paper too.

But did you know that recycling can also be a way to make many other unusual and beautiful things? In many places people are thinking of different and exciting things that they can make from recycled materials.

Paper can be recycled in many different ways. If you look around an office or a kitchen or a bathroom you will probably see different kinds of recycled paper: writing paper, computer paper, and even the pretty paper that we put our presents in.

But recycled paper can be used in more unusual ways too. For example it is sometimes made into a special material to keep houses warm. This material is put inside the roof, and it stops the warm air from the house from escaping through the roof. The people who live in the house stay warmer in winter and they use less electricity to heat their home.

Did you know that paper is also used to make roads? The top part of a road contains recycled paper. It helps to stop road accidents because it makes roads safer in wet weather. It is used at airports too for the same reason. It helps the planes to land safely when the weather is wet.

Some people have found ways of making recycled materials into very beautiful things. In Brazil for example people use recycled paper to make picture frames, containers for flowers, and very beautiful bags.

In London every year in the spring people can visit the Ideal Home Show. Here businesses show people the different things that they make for their homes and gardens. Thousands of visitors come every year to look at furniture, carpets, and pictures and many other things.

In 2006 there was something new for visitors to see at the Ideal Home show. It was called Recycle Now Alley, and everything there was made of recycled materials. There was an office rubbish bin made of . . . office waste paper! There were kitchen cupboards with doors made of recycled plastic cups and the tops of the cupboards were made of very small pieces of glass in many different colours. They looked beautiful and very modern.

Recycle Now Alley also showed many beautiful drinking

Recycle Now Alley

Recycled
leather belts

glasses and glass bowls and plates. You could buy them in different colours – green and blue and red – and they were very popular. And they were also made of recycled glass.

Many people enjoyed looking at the jewellery in Recycle Now Alley. They bought rings made of recycled plastic bags and other pieces of jewellery made of recycled glass. There were bags too – fashionable shoulder bags made of recycled leather belts, and large shopping bags made of recycled plastic and recycled cotton. Everybody loved the modern-looking coffee table. It was red and orange and yellow, and it looked very strong. It was surprising to find out that this big, strong table was made of recycled paper!

Exciting kinds of recycling are happening in many parts of the world. Japan, for example, has a big problem with rubbish. It is a country which loves packaging. But it is also a country where people have always enjoyed making things. Japanese people are often very good at making things out of paper, and now they are good at making things out of recycled paper too.

Is it possible to make a building out of recycled paper? A Japanese architect began to do this in 1995. Shigeru Ban has always hated throwing things away. One day he was looking at some old paper tubes that he had in his office, and he noticed that they were very light and very strong. Perhaps, he thought, he could use paper tubes to make buildings. He went to visit the managers of paper factories and asked them, 'Is it possible to make paper stronger? Is it possible to make paper which can last a long time? Can we make a special kind of paper which can stop fire and water?' The managers decided to try and make the kind of paper that Ban wanted.

They worked hard and made a new kind of strong paper out of old recycled paper. Ban used tubes of this strong paper to make buildings – houses, churches, theatres, and libraries. And now Ban's wonderful buildings are in many countries – Japan, of course, but also France, China, Germany, and the USA.

And there are more good ideas coming from Japan. Hirohiko Fukushima lives in Tokyo. He wants people to grow more trees and make Tokyo greener. As part of his job, he gives people small trees and asks them to plant them. But he used to put his little trees into plastic pots. People threw away the plastic pots and the pots went to landfill sites. Then he had a better idea. He began to make special pots from recycled newspaper, and he also asked offices in Tokyo to give him their old paper. Now he has enough recycled paper to make 5,000 pots each month. The paper pots are put into the ground with the little trees, and the pots soon disappear into the ground as the little trees grow.

In another part of Japan a group of people work together to make soap from used cooking oil. They get the oil from school kitchens and restaurants, and then they clean it in a special way. The process takes about a week. Yuko Fujita, one of the women from the group, is very happy with her soap. 'It is better for the environment,' she says. 'And it is better for your skin too.'

Many Japanese businesses are now making things out of recycled materials. Factories are using plastic bottles to make pens, bags, even sports clothes and school uniforms.

And artists are beginning to recycle too. A British artist called Andy Goldsworthy does not use new materials for his

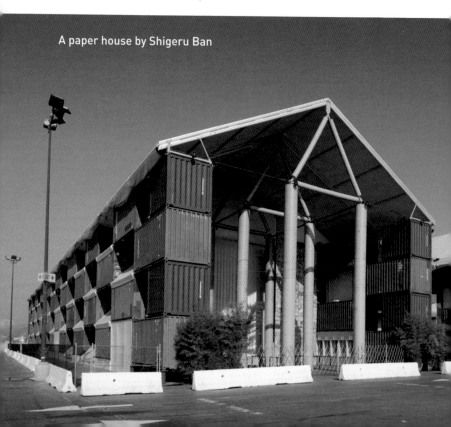

A paper house by Shigeru Ban

work. Instead he uses stones, leaves, ice, sticks, flowers, and other things that he finds to make beautiful pictures and other kinds of art. In New Zealand an artist called Martin Hill also makes art from things he finds around him. Everything he uses comes from the natural world and is returned to it by natural processes. He thinks that factories and businesses should learn to do the same.

Other artists use things that people throw away. A Japanese artist called Yoshiyuki Yamahatsu uses small pieces of coloured plastic from telephone cards. He uses them to make pictures, and each one has about 250,000 pieces in it. Sometimes it takes him a year to make one big picture but he enjoys his work.

An American artist called Jeff Clapp gets his materials

from Mount Everest! Every year hundreds of people climb Mount Everest. The air at the top of the mountain is not very good so climbers take their own air up the mountain in metal bottles. Then they throw the bottles away. Mount Everest is now very untidy, and it is starting to look like a landfill site. But Jeff Clapp uses the empty metal bottles for his work. He makes bells and bowls from them. He also makes shiny balls, which people buy to put on their Christmas trees. So the mountain is cleaner, and rubbish is changed into something beautiful and useful.

In the north of England a furniture business has started using old wood to make new furniture. Each table and chair is made by hand. They are made from wood which factories have thrown away. In London another business takes old furniture from offices and sells it to other people who need it.

All over the world people are thinking of ways to reuse and recycle their rubbish. In the next chapter we will find out more about what different countries are doing.

Jeff Clapp's Everest bells

8   Recycling around the world

Many countries recycle their rubbish, but they do it differently in different places. In this chapter we will travel round the world and see what some of these countries do.

Which country is the best at recycling? If you are driving in Germany and you stop for a rest, you will see recycling bins at all the stopping places. There is one bin for your cans, one for bottles, one for paper, and one for food. So, even when you are travelling, you have to remember to recycle.

People have been recycling in Germany for a long time, and they are very good at it. Every house and flat uses at least five recycling bins, and each bin is a different colour. This helps people to remember where to put different kinds of rubbish and it helps the workers who come to take the rubbish away. The yellow bin is for packaging, the blue bin is for paper, and so on. It is easy when you know the colours.

Batteries and anything else that might contain dangerous chemicals have to go to a recycling centre where people can make them safe. For most people, recycling is not something that they think about – they just do it. Recycling is just a part of their usual way of life, and 90 per cent of German people recycle their rubbish.

Switzerland is another country which is very good at recycling. Swiss people recycle all their glass and paper – they do not throw it away. All kinds of paper and packaging are

Recycling bins in Germany

recycled, not just newspapers. Bottles are recycled too. Of course glass bottles are recycled in many countries, but the Swiss are also good at recycling plastic bottles. In most European countries people only recycle 20 to 40 per cent of their plastic bottles, but in Switzerland they recycle 80 per cent of them.

People recycle nearly everything in Switzerland. When people cut their grass and trees, they put the leaves and pieces of wood outside on the street on one day of the week. This garden rubbish is then taken away and recycled. Old batteries are taken to supermarkets and recycled and there are also special places to recycle aluminium and steel cans.

Why are the Swiss so good at recycling? Maybe it is because in Switzerland recycling is free but throwing away your rubbish is expensive. You have to buy a ticket for each bag of rubbish that you throw away. You put your ticket on the bag of rubbish and the rubbish is taken away. But if you do not buy a ticket, the rubbish will stay outside your house. And it will smell bad!

The Netherlands is another country that is very good at recycling – they recycle everything from shoes to computers. Shoes are left out on the street for recycling, and computers are taken back to the factories where they were made. There they are broken into different small parts and these parts are used again to make new computers.

Big cities always have a lot of rubbish, but in many countries people are trying to think of ways to manage it better. In Paris there are recycling bins near to people's houses and flats. Parisians do not have to go to supermarkets to recycle their rubbish, because they can do it in their own street.

Recycling bins in Paris

In many countries people in towns are given their own recycling bins, but sometimes there is a problem. People do not always want to recycle their rubbish – they think it is too difficult. In Newcastle upon Tyne, in the north of England, there was a big problem. Everybody had recycling bins but

Recycling art

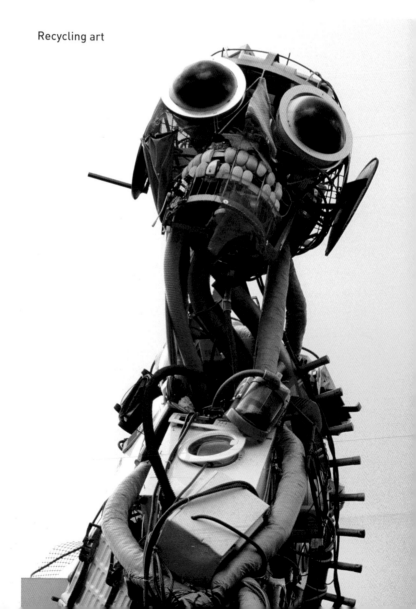

only a few people were using them. Nobody knew what the answer was, but then somebody had an idea.

'Let's make it a game. People like to win money. Maybe they can win money if they recycle their rubbish.'

Tickets with numbers on them were put on every recycling bin in Newcastle. When the bins were used, the numbers went into a computer. At the end of each month the computer chose a number. The people who had that number on their recycling bin won a lot of money. After that everybody wanted to win the money, and they all started recycling their rubbish in the special bins!

There are other countries where you can make money from recycling too. In Finland you can put your empty plastic bottles or cans into special recycling bins in the centre of towns and villages. A machine inside the bin gives you a ticket. When you have got plenty of tickets, you can get some money. These machines were first used in Finland but now they are used in other Scandinavian countries too. Maybe it is not surprising that Scandinavians recycle more than 60 per cent of their rubbish.

Some European countries are not so successful. Italy does not recycle much, especially in the south, but some people are trying to change this. Some young people in Milan work together to sell used electrical machines like computers on the Internet and on the streets. They use the money that they get from this to teach people about recycling. Some big businesses in Italy are also trying to recycle computers. But Italy only recycles about 15 per cent of its computers.

In Greece the problem is even worse. Every year one billion plastic water bottles and two billion other bottles are thrown away. People throw away their rubbish because they do not know about recycling. If you walk along the streets in

Recycling
fashion

Athens, you will probably never see a recycling bin. Yet there is one very big recycling factory in Athens. It is the biggest recycling factory in Europe and it was built next to a landfill site. But it is never used. Why not? Because a big mountain of rubbish from the landfill site fell on top of it and damaged it.

Recycling is sometimes difficult but it can also be fun. In Bristol in the west of England they had a special 'Waste not' festival. There were games and songs about recycling and people could buy things made of recycled materials. 'Before you bin it, think what's in it', people were told.

In Japan the government is worried because many Japanese landfill sites are nearly full. Some cities are now making people pay for their rubbish so people are throwing away much less rubbish than before. Children are learning about recycling at school and Japanese businesses are selling clothes and furniture made out of recycled materials. Japan is changing fast.

The USA recycles about 30 per cent of its waste. Twenty years ago there was only one recycling centre in the whole country, but ten years later there were more than 20,000, and this number is growing every year. But what do Americans think about recycling? The answer is not clear. America has fifty states and many different ways of living. An American living in Alaska, Wyoming, or Montana is probably not very interested in recycling. These states only recycle 9 per cent of their rubbish. But Americans who live in New York, Virginia, and some other states are probably much more interested. They recycle nearly 50 per cent of their rubbish. If you want to find the best recycling state in America you will have to visit California. San Francisco in California has a zero waste policy.

This idea started in Canberra, the capital of Australia, in 1996. The people of Canberra decided to have a zero waste policy by the year 2010. This means that by that time they will stop putting any rubbish into landfill sites, and instead they will recycle or reuse everything. People in New Zealand were also interested in this idea, because they were already recycling a lot of their rubbish. Now they plan to have a zero waste policy by 2015 for all of the country.

Other places followed. The city of Bath in the south-west

Building walls with recycled cans

of England has a zero waste policy. In the north-east of England, a group called Ban Waste has its own website where people can learn more about zero waste policies in different countries.

So where can you go in the world to find the place that recycles the most and throws away the least? The answer is Africa. If you go to a small village in Senegal, for example, you will find cups made of cans, shoes made of car tyres, and schoolbooks covered with old newspapers to keep them clean. Food is not wasted. If any part of a fruit or vegetable is not eaten, it is given to the goats and chickens. Old cars and bicycles are used to make or mend newer ones. Metal waste is used to make bowls and plates and useful things for cooking. Sometimes it is used to make children's toys too. Maybe this is real zero waste.

So after travelling around the world, perhaps it is time to go back home. The next chapter will show you how *you* can recycle more and throw away less.

9   What can you do?

Can one person help to make the world cleaner? Can you do anything about the mountains of rubbish that are getting bigger every day?

The answer is yes. You can help. There are things that everybody can do. But where do you start?

Perhaps the best time to begin is when you go shopping. Before you leave your house, pick up some bags to take with you. If you take some bags to the shop, you will not need to bring any more bags home with you. Did you know that most people bring home at least ten new plastic bags a week from their visits to the shops? It is a good idea to take plastic bags to the supermarket with you, but it is an even better

Take your own bag when you go shopping

Try to avoid packaging

idea to carry bags made of stronger material. They do not break easily so you can keep them for a long time. Also bags made of cotton and other natural materials are much better in landfill sites than plastic.

So after you have arrived at the shopping centre with your own bags, what else can you do? The answer is to choose carefully. Try to buy things that you can keep for a long time. Do not buy things that are used once and then thrown away like cheap cameras and plastic cups. Look for glass bottles instead of plastic ones.

Think about clothes in the same way. Fashions change very quickly, and something which is fashionable this year will look out of date next year. Cheap clothes are often made of cheap material too, and you have to throw them away more quickly. It is better to buy a few well-made clothes than a lot of cheap, badly-made ones.

When you buy fruit and vegetables, it is not worth paying for a lot of plastic packaging. Do bananas need to be in a plastic bag? Bananas already have a coat – their own banana skin. What about apples? Do they need to be in a group of four on a black plastic plate with a plastic cover? It is better to choose the apples you want and put them into your own bag. In Britain 33 per cent of the rubbish that people throw away every week is packaging.

Finally, look for recycled paper and other recycled things when you go shopping. When you buy things made of recycled paper, plastic and other materials, you are helping to pay for recycling.

So you are careful with your shopping, and you try to avoid packaging, but there are still things in your house that you need to throw away. Or do you?

Maybe there are other things that you can do. Remember, something that you don't want any more may be useful for somebody else. Perhaps you can sell it in a shop or on the Internet. Maybe you can just give it away. There are shops that will sell your old clothes and books and use the money that they get to help poor or sick people. Old clothes are also fun for children to use in their games. They like to wear adults' clothes and shoes.

Think about using things in a different way. A big bed sheet can be used again to make smaller sheets for a baby's bed. Even very old and damaged clothes can still be used for cleaning your furniture and windows. And when you cannot find anything useful to do with old clothes, make sure that you put them in recycling bins, not in ordinary rubbish bins. Then they can be used to make other clothes or paper.

Paper can also be used more than once. Keep a box beside your computer at work or at home and put used paper into

There are shops that will sell your old clothes

it. Make sure that everybody uses both sides of the paper before they recycle it.

Plastic bags can be used many times for shopping, and you can also use them in other ways. Put some in your suitcase when you go on holiday. They will be useful when you buy presents. You can also use them to put dirty clothes in at the end of the holiday. Push several bags inside big envelopes when you are posting things that could break. And a plastic bag inside a bin will keep it clean.

You can fill up plastic bottles and use them again many times, but you must wash them well. In hot weather you can make ice in them. You can put bottles of iced water in a bag to keep your sandwiches cold if you are going on a long journey or eating on the beach.

If you enjoy growing plants, there are many things that you can do with plastic bottles. For example, when you go on holiday, you can fill plastic bottles with water, make very small holes in them, and then put them near your plants. They will give water to the plants while you are away.

Cut large plastic bottles in half. You can use them in the garden to cover plants when the weather is cold. Or you can grow very small baby plants inside them. You can also do this with plastic cups.

If you have a garden, you can tie big empty plastic bottles onto trees or sticks, and they will move in the wind and frighten the birds. This will keep the birds away from your fruit or vegetables. But if you like the birds and want them

Using plastic bottles in the garden

to visit your garden, you can make a wooden bird table and cut the plastic bottles to make small cups. Put food for the birds inside these cups and tie them to the bird table.

Finally, remember that schools can use a lot of the things that people call 'rubbish'. Big boxes, small boxes, egg boxes, birthday cards, magazines, pieces of material and shiny paper can all be fun for younger children. They are often used to make pictures and strange animals and extraordinary machines. If you live near a school, ask the teachers what kind of things they need.

So perhaps you cannot save the environment by yourself, but there are many things that one person can do. More and more people are talking about these things and making changes in their lives. Perhaps in this way we can help to make the rubbish mountains smaller.

10   The future

We cannot be sure what will happen in the future but we do know that things are changing now. In many countries of the world people are saying, 'We must do something about our rubbish. We don't want our world to become one big landfill site.'

In Germany when people go to the supermarket they usually leave all the packaging in the shop when they pay for their shopping. They only take the packaging that they need, which is not very much.

In Ireland the government were very worried about plastic bags so they decided to make people pay for them. Since 2002 Irish people have been paying for any plastic bags they take home from the shops. Of course, they soon stopped buying new bags and started taking bags with them when they went to the shops. Many other countries are now doing the same thing.

Some countries have made even bigger changes. In 2006 the people of Zanzibar decided to stop making plastic bags. They were worried because the plastic bags looked ugly and they were killing fish and sea animals. They also said that nobody could bring plastic bags into the country. Soon there were no plastic bags in Zanzibar.

A city in Brazil has made some very exciting changes. In Curitiba two-thirds of the city's rubbish is recycled. Poor people bring their rubbish to a recycling place and they are given bus tickets and food. The rubbish is taken to a special factory which is made of recycled materials. The workers at this factory are people who have had big problems in their lives but now they have jobs. They sort the rubbish into cans, glass, plastic, and paper, and everything is recycled. Curitiba is a clean city. Perhaps in the future other cities will be as clean as Curitiba.

Sometimes changes come from ordinary people, not from governments. One of the most exciting recycling ideas is Freecycle. This is a big idea that has grown around the world. People join a Freecycle group because they are looking for things or have things that they want to give to other people. Perhaps they have a chair that they do not need any more, or they want a camera. They leave a message on the computer to tell people what they want or what they are going to give. Nobody buys or sells anything – people give things to other

Recycling in Curitiba, Brazil

people who want them. It is a good idea because it recycles useful things and helps people to give away things that they do not want.

How big is Freecycle? It is extraordinarily large. It started in 2003 and there are now groups in more than 50 countries all around the world, from Finland to Argentina, from Ethiopia to Venezuela, from Korea to Kuwait. Look on the Internet to find out if your country has Freecycle groups.

Businesses are beginning to have new ideas as well. Factories are making more and more things from recycled materials. They are also making new kinds of supermarket bags which are not made of plastic. They are made of natural materials, which look like plastic but are better for the Earth.

The big supermarkets are also starting to change their ideas. In the UK in 2005 the thirteen biggest supermarkets and shops made a promise. They said that in the next five years they will stop using so much packaging.

Will they keep their promise? Perhaps they will because the government also made a new law. If businesses use too much packaging, they will have to pay a lot of money.

Martin Hill's
Stone Circle

Recycling is important and sometimes it is exciting too, but it is only one part of the answer. Using less and reusing are also important answers to the problem of rubbish.

In the twentieth century we saw the beginning of the throwaway world. Perhaps in the twenty-first century we will see the end of it.

GLOSSARY

aluminium a light metal of a silver colour

architect a person who designs and plans buildings

art beautiful things like paintings and drawings that somebody
  has made; **artist** a person who makes works of art

ash the grey powder that is left after something has burned

battery something that makes electricity for a clock, radio etc

bin a container for rubbish

can a metal container for food or drink

cart a wooden vehicle with wheels, usually pulled by a horse

chemical something solid or liquid used in chemistry

collect to go somewhere to get things and take them away

compost (*n & v*) a material that is made from rotted plants and
  food and that is used to help plants grow

Earth the world

electricity power that can make heat and light

environment the air, water, land, animals, and plants around us

especially more than usual or more than others

frame a thin piece of wood or metal around the edge of a
  picture

goat an animal with horns that gives milk

government a group of people who control a country

Internet the international network of computers that lets you
  see information from all over the world

jewellery beautiful things that you wear on your ears, fingers etc

last (*v*) to continue for a time

law one of the rules of a country; **break the law** to do something
  that the law does not allow

liquid water, oil, and milk are all liquids

material what you use for making or doing something

mobile phone a phone that you can carry with you and use
  anywhere

ordinary not strange or special

packaging   all the materials – paper, plastic etc – that are put around things that you buy

pig   an animal with pink skin and short legs, kept on farms for its meat

plastic   a light strong material used to make many different things

policy   a plan that people agree to follow

process   a number of actions, one after the other, for doing or making something

room   enough space to do something

satellite dish   something that you put on the outside of your house so you can receive television pictures from a satellite

soap   something that you use with water for washing and cleaning

sort (*v*)   to put things into groups

steel   a strong hard metal used to make things like knives

tonne   one thousand kilos

toxic   containing things that will hurt or kill animals or people

toy   a thing for a child to play with

tube   a long thin pipe

turtle   an animal that lives in the sea and has a hard shell on its back

waste   things that are not wanted or needed

website   a place on the Internet where you can find out information about something

Recycling

ACTIVITIES

ACTIVITIES

Before Reading

1 **What can you make from these recycled things? Can you guess?**

From recycled . . .	you can make . . .
1 drinks cans	a fuel for cars
2 plastic bottles	b buildings
3 cooking oil	c jewellery
4 glass	d toys
5 paper	e clothes

2 **Do you agree with these statements?**
Tick YES or NO.

	YES	NO
1 Recycling is a waste of time.	☐	☐
2 We can all do something to help recycling.	☐	☐
3 People will only recycle if they are paid to do it.	☐	☑
4 In my country we should do more to recycle.	☑	☐
5 People need to learn about recycling when they are young.	☑	☐

3 **Now think about the answers to these questions.**

1 Which country is the best at recycling?
2 What are the most difficult things to recycle? *plastic*
3 What do you know about recycling in your country?

ACTIVITIES

While Reading

Read Chapter 1 and decide if the sentences are true (T) or false (F). Change the false sentences into true ones.

1 When people throw away rubbish they don't usually think T about it any more.
2 There are plenty of landfill sites for us to use in the future. F
3 In the UK each person throws away more than a thousand T plastic bags every year.
4 The smell from burning rubbish can make people ill. T
5 Toxic waste contains dangerous metals or chemicals. T
6 These days, poor countries are happy to take toxic waste from rich countries.
7 Rubbish is a problem for both rich countries and poor T countries.
8 There is no rubbish in any part of Mexico.

Read Chapter 2. Choose the best question word for these questions, and then answer them.

What / Which / Where / Why

1 _____ were the earliest landfill sites found?
2 _____ is compost used for?
3 _____ did people in London use to wear high wooden shoes?
4 _____ was Shakespeare's father punished in 1515?
5 _____ people take away much of Cairo's rubbish?
6 _____ is your life like if you live near a landfill site?
7 _____ in the Philippines did a hill of rubbish fall down?
8 _____ did people continue to live and work there?

Read Chapter 3 and then answer these questions.

1 Why is there more rubbish today than in the past?
2 Why do businesses change the shape or colour of things like mobile phones so often?
3 How does packaging make people buy more?
4 How much of the rubbish in the United States can be recycled?
5 How have the lives of people in China changed in the last twenty years?
6 Why can't the UK make more landfill sites?
7 What did people use ash for in the past?
8 What is different about recycling today?

Read Chapters 4 and 5 and match the two halves of theses sentences.

1 Many of the things we throw away . . .
2 Different kinds of glass . . .
3 Although it is good to recycle paper . . .
4 Americans are recycling more paper, . . .
5 Recycling metal saves money because . . .
6 Aluminium and steel . . .
7 Things made of plastic . . .
8 Plastic can be recycled but . . .

a) but they are using more too.
b) are both easy to recycle.
c) making new metal is expensive.
d) it is not easy to do.
e) can last for more than 400 years.
f) it is better to use less of it.
g) can be used again.
h) can't be recycled together.

Read Chapter 6 and then complete these sentences with the correct words or phrases.

batteries, computers, fridges, mobile phones, vegetable oil

1 _____ are useful in countries where there aren't many telephone lines.
2 Old _____ can be mended and sent to poorer countries.
3 _____ must be recycled in European countries in future.
4 Some radios and lights can work without _____ .
5 Cars can burn _____ in their engines.

Read Chapter 7 and match the people, the materials, and the things that they made.

	USED ...	TO MAKE ...
Shigeru Ban	leaves, sticks, and flowers	pots for plants
Hirohiko Fukushima		bells
Andy Goldsworthy	telephone cards	big pictures
Yoshiyuki Yamahatsu	metal bottles	pictures and other art
Jeff Clapp	paper tubes	
	newspaper	buildings

Read Chapter 8. Here are some untrue sentences. Change them into true sentences.

1 German bins have different shapes for different kinds of rubbish.
2 Throwing away rubbish in Switzerland is free.
3 People in the Netherlands leave their computers out on the street for recycling.
4 In Finland you pay money when you recycle a lot of rubbish.
5 There are many recycling bins in Athens.
6 Japanese children learn about recycling at home.
7 Alaska is the best recycling state in the USA.

Read Chapter 9. Then circle the correct words and phrases to complete these sentences.

1 It's best to take *cotton / plastic* bags to the supermarket.

2 Buy things that *last a long time / can be thrown away quickly.*

3 Fruit *needs / doesn't need* a lot of packaging.

4 If you have clothes you don't want any more, you can *give / throw* them away.

5 Plastic bags *are only useful for shopping / can be used for many things.*

6 When you use plastic bottles again, you must *wash them well / cut them up.*

7 *Schools / Hospitals* can use old boxes and cards to make interesting things.

8 You *can / can't* save the environment by yourself.

Read Chapter 10 and answer these questions.

1 Why are people worried about rubbish?

2 When the Irish government were worried about plastic bags, what did they do?

3 Why did the people of Zanzibar decide to stop using plastic bags?

4 Which city in Brazil is trying interesting new ways of recycling?

5 Why do people join a Freecycle group?

6 How many countries have Freecycle groups?

7 What did UK supermarkets promise to do in 2005?

8 When did the 'throwaway world' begin?

ACTIVITIES

After Reading

1 Use the clues below to complete this crossword with words from the story. Then find the hidden words in the crossword.

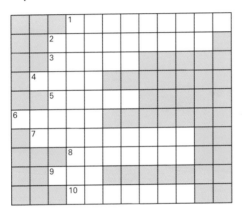

1 What goes around the things that you buy.
2 A light silver-coloured metal.
3 The world we live in.
4 To continue for a time.
5 A strong hard metal.
6 Dangerous to animals and people.
7 A person who designs buildings.
8 A clock or radio can get electricity from this.
9 A metal container for drinks.
10 This country is very good at recycling.

The hidden words are _____ .

2 Complete this report about Freecycle, using the words below.

computers, governments, groups, home, information, Internet, messages, need, ordinary, recycles, rubbish, selling, world

Freecycle was started by _____ people, not by _____, and it _____ things that people don't want any more. There's no buying or _____ on Freecycle. People use their _____ to send _____ to each other, saying what they have or what they _____. So things that people don't want any more go to a new _____ instead of going in the _____. You can find Freecycle _____ all over the _____. If you look on the _____, you can find out more _____ about Freecycle.

3 Do you think these things will happen by 2050? Write A, B, C, D, or E next to each sentence.

A = YES

B = PROBABLY

C = MAYBE

D = PROBABLY NOT

E = NO

1 No one will use plastic bags any more.
2 Rubbish will be sent to the Moon.
3 Most cars and buses will use electricity.
4 Fruit and vegetables will not have packaging.
5 All drinks will come in glass bottles.
6 New houses will have to be made of recycled materials.
7 The more rubbish you make, the more you will have to pay.

Now add two more things you think will be true in the year 2050, and say why you think this.

4 What can we do about plastic bags? Here are some ideas.
   Discuss which are the best, and give your reasons.

   • Give shoppers a recyclable bag which they can use again
     and again.
   • Make shoppers pay for plastic bags.
   • Use bags made from recyclable material.
   • Make supermarkets pay for recycling plastic bags.
   • Make it easy for shoppers to recycle old plastic bags.
   • Give shoppers a small amount of money when they use
     their own bags.
   • Add your own ideas to this list.

   The website www.reusablebags.com has more ideas in the
   part called 'Take Action'.

5 Choose something that interests you about recycling. Find
   some more information about it, and make a poster or give a
   talk to your class. Here are some ideas.

   • Write a report on the rubbish that your family (or class,
     or place of work) makes in one week. What can you do to
     recycle more?
   • Design a bag with a recycling message that shoppers can
     use.
   • Talk to an older person about recycling in the past. What
     was different then? What did people do before there were
     plastic bags? What could we learn from this?

   There is lots of information on the Internet. Two helpful
   websites are www.recyclenow.com and
   www.en.wikipedia.org/wiki/Recycling

ABOUT THE AUTHOR

Sue Stewart has been teaching English for more than twenty-five years. She has taught in France, Sudan and Senegal, but she now lives and works in Newcastle upon Tyne in the north-east of England. She is married and has two children and two cats.

Her main job is teaching but she has also written many different kinds of English language course materials. These include health and safety training material for people learning English who work in hospitals. Her speciality is writing about accidents in hospital corridors, and she even wrote the script for a film about an accident on a wet floor in a hospital.

She enjoys meeting people from different countries and finding out how they live, which was very useful for this book. She has been keen on recycling for a long time, but it was only when she started writing this book that she really understood how important it was and started telling other people about it. Her aim now is to recycle everything and have a completely empty rubbish bin but she hasn't quite managed that yet.

In her spare time she enjoys playing badminton and walking. She also belongs to a book group and enjoys talking about books with her friends.

OXFORD BOOKWORMS LIBRARY

Classics • Crime & Mystery • Factfiles • Fantasy & Horror
Human Interest • Playscripts • Thriller & Adventure
True Stories • World Stories

The OXFORD BOOKWORMS LIBRARY provides enjoyable reading in English, with a wide range of classic and modern fiction, non-fiction, and plays. It includes original and adapted texts in seven carefully graded language stages, which take learners from beginner to advanced level. An overview is given on the next pages.

All Stage 1 titles are available as audio recordings, as well as over eighty other titles from Starter to Stage 6. All Starters and many titles at Stages 1 to 4 are specially recommended for younger learners. Every Bookworm is illustrated, and Starters and Factfiles have full-colour illustrations.

The OXFORD BOOKWORMS LIBRARY also offers extensive support. Each book contains an introduction to the story, notes about the author, a glossary, and activities. Additional resources include tests and worksheets, and answers for these and for the activities in the books. There is advice on running a class library, using audio recordings, and the many ways of using Oxford Bookworms in reading programmes. Resource materials are available on the website <www.oup.com/bookworms>.

The *Oxford Bookworms Collection* is a series for advanced learners. It consists of volumes of short stories by well-known authors, both classic and modern. Texts are not abridged or adapted in any way, but carefully selected to be accessible to the advanced student.

You can find details and a full list of titles in the *Oxford Bookworms Library Catalogue* and *Oxford English Language Teaching Catalogues*, and on the website <www.oup.com/bookworms>.

THE OXFORD BOOKWORMS LIBRARY
GRADING AND SAMPLE EXTRACTS

STARTER • 250 HEADWORDS

present simple – present continuous – imperative –
can/cannot, must – *going to* (future) – simple gerunds …

Her phone is ringing – but where is it?

Sally gets out of bed and looks in her bag. No phone.
She looks under the bed. No phone. Then she looks behind
the door. There is her phone. Sally picks up her phone and
answers it. *Sally's Phone*

STAGE 1 • 400 HEADWORDS

… past simple – coordination with *and*, *but*, *or* –
subordination with *before*, *after*, *when*, *because*, *so* …

I knew him in Persia. He was a famous builder and I
worked with him there. For a time I was his friend, but
not for long. When he came to Paris, I came after him –
I wanted to watch him. He was a very clever, very dangerous
man. *The Phantom of the Opera*

STAGE 2 • 700 HEADWORDS

… present perfect – *will* (future) – *(don't) have to, must not, could* –
comparison of adjectives – simple *if* clauses – past continuous –
tag questions – *ask/tell* + infinitive …

While I was writing these words in my diary, I decided
what to do. I must try to escape. I shall try to get down the
wall outside. The window is high above the ground, but
I have to try. I shall take some of the gold with me – if I
escape, perhaps it will be helpful later. *Dracula*

STAGE 3 • 1000 HEADWORDS

… should, may – present perfect continuous – *used to* – past perfect
– causative – relative clauses – indirect statements …

Of course, it was most important that no one should see
Colin, Mary, or Dickon entering the secret garden. So Colin
gave orders to the gardeners that they must all keep away
from that part of the garden in future. *The Secret Garden*

STAGE 4 • 1400 HEADWORDS

… past perfect continuous – passive (simple forms) –
would conditional clauses – indirect questions –
relatives with *where/when* – gerunds after prepositions/phrases …

I was glad. Now Hyde could not show his face to the world
again. If he did, every honest man in London would be proud
to report him to the police. *Dr Jekyll and Mr Hyde*

STAGE 5 • 1800 HEADWORDS

… future continuous – future perfect –
passive (modals, continuous forms) –
would have conditional clauses – modals + perfect infinitive …

If he had spoken Estella's name, I would have hit him. I was so
angry with him, and so depressed about my future, that I could
not eat the breakfast. Instead I went straight to the old house.
Great Expectations

STAGE 6 • 2500 HEADWORDS

… passive (infinitives, gerunds) – advanced modal meanings –
clauses of concession, condition

When I stepped up to the piano, I was confident. It was as if I
knew that the prodigy side of me really did exist. And when I
started to play, I was so caught up in how lovely I looked that
I didn't worry how I would sound. *The Joy Luck Club*

BOOKWORMS · FACTFILES · STAGE 3

Australia and New Zealand

CHRISTINE LINDOP

What do you find in these two countries at the end of the world? One is an enormous island, where only twenty million people live – and the other is two long, narrow islands, with ten sheep for every person. One country has the biggest rock in all the world, and a town where everybody lives under the ground; the other has a beach where you can sit beside the sea in a pool of hot water, and lakes that are bright yellow, green, and blue. Open this book and start your journey – to two countries where something strange, beautiful or surprising waits around every corner.

BOOKWORMS · FACTFILES · STAGE 3

Information Technology

PAUL A. DAVIES

It is hard to imagine the modern world without information technology. At home, at work, and at play, mobile phones, e-mails and computers have become part of daily life.

The story of information technology is a story of machines – from the ancient abacus to the small powerful computer chips of today. But it is also a story of people. Meet a woman who wrote computer programs two hundred years ago, a teenage millionaire, a man who began with a paperclip and ended with a house – and the criminals who want your name and your money.

Come and discover the world of information technology.